THE HEYDAY OF THE **WESTERNS**
DEREK HUNTRISS

Ian Allan
PUBLISHING

Introduction

First published 2003

ISBN 0 7110 2981 4

All rights reserved. No part of this book may be reproduced or transmitted in any form or by any means, electronic or mechanical, including photocopying, recording or by any information storage and retrieval system, without permission from the Publisher in writing.

© Derek Huntriss 2003

Published by Ian Allan Publishing

an imprint of Ian Allan Publishing Ltd, Hersham, Surrey KT12 4RG.
Printed by Ian Allan Printing Ltd, Hersham, Surrey KT12 4RG.

Code: 0309/B2

Front cover: Green-liveried D1035 *Western Yeoman* is observing the 40mph permanent way restriction as it approaches Aynho Junction on 29 August 1962 with the 11.40am Birkenhead (Woodside) to Paddington. *M. Mensing*

Rear cover: Only weeks out of works, newly constructed D1062 *Western Courier* approaches Acocks Green station, Birmingham, with the 3.10pm Paddington to Wolverhampton (Low Level) on 11 June 1963. *M. Mensing*

Title page: No D1005 *Western Venturer* powers through Dawlish Warren with 1A85, the Saturdays only 17.40 Paignton to Paddington, on 19 May 1974. *Les Folkard*

Constructed as a replacement for the 'King' class 4-6-0 and a significant improvement on the performance of a D800 'Warship', the first of the C-C 2,700hp 'Western' class diesel-hydraulics commenced trials from Swindon in February 1962. The Western Regions (WR)'s decision to stand alone and opt for diesel-hydraulics has been debated long and hard in books and magazines for many years. It is not the author's remit to add fuel to the argument but to offer the reader a strong selection of colour images recalling the life of the 'Westerns' in their heyday.

Initially 'Western' performance was mediocre. At the start of the 1962-63 winter timetable they replaced the 'Kings' on the Paddington to Birmingham/Wolverhampton expresses with correspondingly accelerated schedules — but the failure rate was high, the running disappointing and, adding insult to injury, there was an outbreak of metal fatigue in the axles. In addition to the excessive flange wear suffered by the 'Warships' the WR temporarily imposed an overall 80mph speed restriction.

With the takeover by the London Midland Region of the former GWR route north of Banbury, the Birmingham line was invaded by Brush Type 4s, the 'Westerns' being transferred to the South Wales line and to the West of England route with which they were primarily associated and it is perhaps fitting that during their last years on the WR they were all stationed at Laira.

By the summer of 1965 the WR had gained sufficient confidence in the class to return the maximum speed limit to 90mph and accelerate both the Bristol and West of England services, together with those to South Wales. From that year the 'Westerns' went from strength to strength and like so many diesel types their performance improved as time passed, the crews becoming better acquainted with the driving techniques. Adding to these factors, there were better maintenance and improvements to the design itself.

Of all the WR diesel-hydraulics it was the 'Westerns' that commanded massive enthusiast support, this being reflected in the relatively large number of locomotives preserved.

Bibliography

A. N. Curtis: *Cast of Thousands;* A & C Services
A. N. Curtis: *Western Dawn;* A & C Services
A. N. Curtis: *Western Liveries;* A & C Services
Magazines:
Backtrack; Modern Railways; Railway Magazine; Railway World; Trains Illustrated; RCTS – The Railway Observer

Acknowledgments

Most railway photographers reserved their film for steam survivors and colour pictures of early diesels are scarce. I am indebted to all those who contributed irreplaceable transparencies for inclusion in this book. We all owe them our sincere thanks for recording a period fast becoming as remote as the steam age itself.

Derek Huntriss
Coventry
July 2003

It is now over a quarter of a century since the last diesel-hydraulic was used in revenue-earning service on BR when the 'Warships', 'Westerns' and 'Hymeks' were swept aside by the advent of the HST and other later designs of diesel in much the same way as they had ousted the 'Castles' and 'Kings' at the end of the steam era. Reminding us of the heyday of the 'Westerns' this splendid view shows standard coach maroon-liveried No D1008 *Western Harrier* as its heads a rake of matching coloured coaching stock which forms the up 'Cambrian Coast Express near Acocks Green, Birmingham on 17 September 1962. The distinctive coach maroon livery carried on some non-steam traction was based on that of the 1956 BR carriage colours and was only applied to 'Westerns' and the slightly older 'Warships' and was chosen in preference to the near-GWR green livery. No D1008 had the distinction of being what was believed to be the first WR diesel-hydraulic to work onto the Eastern Region when it travelled to Peterborough East with a football supporters excursion from Swindon on Easter Monday 1963. *M. Mensing*

Above: This view taken in 'A' shop at Swindon Works on 27 January 1963 shows a 'Western' (D1025 is written in chalk on the frames) in the first stages of construction alongside steam locomotives which are under repair. Having gained much experience with the building of the D800s, both technical and artisan staff at Swindon Works had amassed what was acknowledged to be the greatest collective knowledge of stressed-skin construction available at any workshop on BR. Entering traffic some 10 months later in November 1963, No D1025 *Western Guardsman* was first allocated to Cardiff. *T. B. Owen*

Right: Another view taken inside 'A' shop at Swindon Works shows D1011 *Western Thunderer* under repair on 14 November 1971. Constructed as part of Lot 450 *Western Thunderer* was completed in October 1962 and subsequently allocated to Old Oak Common depot. No D1011 had carried the initial maroon livery but from November 1966 the 'Westerns' began to receive the new standard livery of Rail Blue with full yellow ends — the class carrying this livery better than many other BR diesel types. *Terry Nicholls*

Left: This detail view taken at Swindon Works on 22 March 1964 shows D1015 *Western Champion* under repair with its bogie removed. Whilst the WR continued to deliberate about the future new livery for its 'Western' hydraulics, the final experiment was to paint D1015 in Golden Ochre or, to be precise, Stroudley's 'Improved Engine Green' for the London, Brighton and South Coast Railway (LBSCR). This experiment followed a suggestion by Brian Haresnape and George Williams of the British Transport Commission Design Office. Without the LBSCR's elaborate lining out this colour looked rather insipid and was not applied to any further 'Westerns' — the colour scheme was also applied to a Brush Type 2 on the Eastern Region where a similar lack of favour was expressed. *T. B. Owen*

Right: Although officially withdrawn and destined for preservation, D1062 *Western Courier* is seen on display outside Swindon Works at its Open Day on 13 September 1975. For some months the locomotive had been displayed on the works' turntable and, being in reasonably sound condition, a successful bid was made by the Western Locomotive Association. After the fitting of newly-overhauled engines and a full repaint in maroon livery the locomotive was moved to Newton Abbot to join four other withdrawn 'Westerns' also stored pending preservation. *Hugh Ballantyne*

Completed in September 1962 D1009 *Western Invader* is seen outside the shed at Swindon. One of the first duties undertaken by D1009 was made on 4 October 1962 when it took an afternoon parcels working from Swindon to Cardiff, making what was believed to be the class's first incursion into South Wales, from where it returned light engine. Once trials were completed D1009 was allocated to Old Oak Common. *Raymond Reed*

With red background to its numberplates and small yellow warning panels, newly constructed D1003 *Western Pioneer* is seen outside Swindon Works on 14 April 1962. One week later, harnessed to D1002 *Western Pathfinder*, D1003 worked up from Swindon to Paddington on 21 April 1962 with the 6.55am ex-Cheltenham. D1003 returned on the afternoon Plymouth parcels, but D1002 remained in London to begin crew-training and was noted on 24 April working the 7pm Paddington to Didcot semi-fast. Recurrent problems with the locomotive's transmissions delayed full entry into service, maintenance staff complaining of the crowded internal layout.

At that time the WR had organised a questionaire amongst junior enthusiasts seeking their preference of livery, with a free trip on one of the locomotives as a prize. Nearly three hundred entries were received, competitors being asked to vote for Desert Sand, maroon or green — one winner, however, suggested that *Devon* sand might be more appropriate — her address — *Newton Abbot*.

This competition had been little more than a publicity gimmick, the final decision for the introduction of the coach maroon livery being made by Stanley Raymond, WR General Manager.
T. B. Owen

No D1071 *Western Renown* has arrived at the buffer stops at Paddington on 23 May 1975 carrying the headcode 1A45 of the 12.35 ex-Penzance — the photographer's two sons looking on with great interest. The eldest, Stephen, went on to be an HST driver for First Great Western and become the family's fifth generation of railwayman — his forebears serving both the GWR and BR Western Region. At that time the 'Westerns' continued to play a large part in West of England services from London and although not fitted to work air-conditioned stock, '52s' as the 'Westerns' were later classified sometimes found themselves at the head of air-conditioned trains deputising for failed Class 50s or '47/4s'. According to the summer timetable diagrams for 1975 only a handful of Class 52 turns remained on the Paddington to Penzance and Torbay services. These included the 08.30 Paddington to Paignton and 13.55 (SX), 15.55 (SO) return, also the 08.45 Penzance to Paddington, returning with the 16.53 Paddington to Plymouth (FSX) or Penzance (FSO). Added to these were a number of Saturday trains although in practice the class saw much wider use. *Terry Nicholls*

The A40(M) motorway has yet to appear in this view taken near Westbourne Park on 19 October 1963. Steam operations are still in evidence as D1049 *Western Monarch* heads a down Paddington to Birmingham and Wolverhampton express, the stock being made up of a mixed rake of chocolate and cream, maroon and blood and custard liveried Mk I coaches. Only two weeks after this picture was taken, on 4 November 1962, at least half of the class were taken out of service due to transmission failures — initially all locomotives which had covered more than 75,000 miles were dealt with — the remainder being dealt with in time. *R. C. Riley*

Another picture taken on 19 October 1963 shows D1035 *Western Yeoman* passing Subway Junction — the first of four green-liveried 'Westerns' to be outshopped from Crewe. Whilst Swindon was to build 35 locomotives to be numbered D1000 to D1034, the remaining 39, D1035-D1073, were to be built at Crewe. The decision to build at Crewe was taken to minimise delivery delays and distribute new work amongst BR workshops. Although Crewe had never built a diesel-hydraulic or one which used the complex technologies of stressed-skin construction it had a sound record of on-time deliveries and managed to achieve lower production costs than at Swindon. As deliveries continued Crewe Works delivered more rapidly than Swindon, the final five of the Swindon order, D1030-34, being transferred to Crewe. Whilst D1073 was the last in the sequence, D1034 was the last to be built and D1029 was the last to enter traffic. *R. C. Riley*

Contrasting styles in locomotive liveries are evident in this picture taken outside the factory at Old Oak Common on 11 April 1964. In the company of D1023 *Western Fusilier*, resplendent in the maroon livery which was later adopted as standard, is the experimental-liveried D1000 *Western Enterprise*. This is carrying the livery called Desert Sand and judging by the condition of the paintwork was not the most practical of colour schemes. Also evident behind the 'Westerns' are green-liveried 'Hymeks' Nos D7070 and D7087. The new diesel depot at Old Oak Common became fully operational on 20 October 1965 and virtually coincided with the completion of the changeover from steam to diesel traction. The new depot was the last and vital London link in a chain of six major servicing and maintenance centres established at strategic points throughout the Western Region. Throughout the two years of demolition and reconstruction for its new role the depot continued to operate without any major interruption in the supply of locomotives — an outstanding achievement when, at one period, it was serving both steam and diesel traction. A single-storey servicing shed was brought into use in January 1965 and has three through roads, each of which can accommodate two of the largest main-line locomotives. *R. C. Riley*

Above: Desert Sand-liveried 'Western' D1000 *Western Enterprise* is seen inside the depot at Old Oak Common on 12 August 1962. D1000 had reached Laira depot on 28 January 1962, piloting the the 4.15pm Paddington to Plymouth from Bristol. Soon afterwards it was put on a crew-training diagram covering the up 'Mayflower' to Newton Abbot, returning as pilot to a Type 4 on the 12.45am Manchester to Plymouth sleeping car train; it then headed the up 'Royal Duchy' from Plymouth to Newton Abbot and returned to Plymouth piloting the 2.30pm ex-Paddington. *T. B. Owen*

Right: No D1005 *Western Venturer* is seen alongside the depot at Old Oak Common on a very wet day in October 1963. D1005 had been in traffic since June 1962, its first allocation being to Laira depot in Plymouth, subsequent allocation to Old Oak Common taking place in October of that year. Being set to be among the members of the class to survive into 1977, D1005 was withdrawn from traffic on 14 November 1976 following a dynostarter fire, its last revenue earning duty being with the previous day's 6M51 03.00 Westbury to Banbury. *Geoff Rixon*

No D1055 *Western Advocate* is depicted leaving Banbury with the 12.25pm Birmingham New Street to Paddington service on 11 October 1975. Less than three months after this picture was taken on the evening of Friday 2 January 1976 high winds had brought down telegraph poles and trees between Droitwich Spa and Worcester Tunnel signalbox, severing communication. Subsequently Time Interval Working was implemented and had worked satisfactorily through the night. The following morning the driver of D1055 refused to work his booked return train from Bescot to Gloucester because of delays on his outward trip and had insisted on returning light engine. In doing so his locomotive hit the rear of a one-van parcels train (No 31241 and a GUV) admitted into the section 10 minutes earlier. His locomotive collided at speed with the parcels train after its driver had stopped to report its position. The driver and guard travelling in the leading cab of D1055 were both killed. *Bryan Hicks*

This side-on view taken close to Harbury tunnel, on the climb away from Leamington Spa, shows D1010 *Western Campaigner* as it heads the 2.45pm Birkenhead (Woodside) to Paddington on 17 August 1963. However much diesels were deplored by die-hard steam enthusiasts, diesel and electric traction was putting up records over increasingly long distances which would not have been possible even with the most advanced forms of steam motive power. So it was that Saturday 7 May 1966 saw the establishment of yet another record that would have been impossible with steam power. It was the first non-stop run in history over the 305$\frac{1}{4}$ miles from Paddington to Penzance. With the willing and most efficient cooperation of the Western and Southern Region authorities, who did everything in their power to ensure a run without any intermediate stop, D1010 headed a six-coach special train chartered by the Ian Allan organisation. *Mike Mensing*

Monday, 10 September 1962 was the first day of full diesel working on the Paddington to Wolverhampton services via Birmingham (Snow Hill). The inaugural services were given civic send-offs. The 9.0am from Paddington was seen off by the mayor of the borough and arrival at Snow Hill behind D1038 *Western Sovereign* was seven minutes early. In the reverse direction the 7.10am from Shrewsbury was driven by the mayor as far as Snow Hill, where the Lord Mayor of Birmingham entered the cab for a run to Leamington. Unfortunately the trip set aside for the press, the 11.0am from Snow Hill headed by D1000 *Western Enterprise*, suffered delays due to a signal failure at Wednesbury and failure of a previous train at Leamington — arrival at Paddington being 20 minutes late. Here, D1042 *Western Princess* climbs away from Leamington Spa near Whitnash with the 3.30pm Wolverhampton Low Level to Paddington on Sunday, 7 April 1963. *M. Mensing*

Green-liveried D1035 *Western Yeoman* has arrived at the WR Leamington Spa (General) station with an up passenger working on 25 August 1962. At that time Leamington Spa had two passenger stations, General and the former LNWR station, Avenue. A new connection between them was opened on 15 May 1966, the marshalling yard between the stations being lifted and the thrice daily parcels from Nuneaton running directly into General. *H. W. Robinson / J. N. Simms Collection*

Above: Experimental-liveried D1000 *Western Enterprise* waits at Leamington Spa (General) with an up working on 20 July 1963. The first regular rail-road-air service had come into operation on 1 April 1963 and took the form of a feeder service for passengers travelling between the West Midlands and airports throughout the world, via the former GW main line to and from High Wycombe and a motorcoach link between Wycombe and Heathrow. *H. W. Robinson / J.N. Simms Collection*

Right: In the classic setting for up trains at Leamington Spa (General) with the parish church of All Saints forming the backdrop, blue-liveried D1054 *Western Governor* comes to a halt with a Birmingham (New Street) to Paddington express on 9 October 1974. By January 1975 only three Class 52 diagrams to Birmingham remained — the 06.45, 09.05 and 14.05 ex-Paddington with the return workings from New Street at 10.25, 12.25 and 18.25. *Bryan Hicks*

Carefully framed by semaphores at both ends of the train and the station awning, this picture shows D1005 *Western Venturer* arriving at Leamington Spa with an up express working on 3 October 1974. Leamington Spa was also a popular venue for recording the last workings of the 'Westerns' on the Birmingham to Paddington route. Former members of the Lieutenant Pigeon band, Nigel Fletcher and Rob Woodward, had their own recording studio set up for their exploits as musicians and were in an ideal position to record their beloved 'Westerns'. The major problem for this exercise was how to power their equipment. Not wishing to carry their bulky studio items they invested in special outdoor battery equipment. After recording many hydraulics leaving stations they diversified into footplate recordings with special permission from British Railways. Their final product was an album called 'Westerns' which was released by Argo Records on 1 May 1975. *Bryan Hicks*

Maroon-liveried D1001 *Western Pathfinder* climbs the 1 in 108 of Hatton bank with a Paddington to Birmingham and Wolverhampton working on 29 September 1962. With interest in a unified livery for both locomotives and coaching stock, the BTC requested that D1001 be outshopped in standard coach maroon livery with yellow bufferbeams and that the aluminium emblem used on D1000 be replaced with a standard coaching stock cypher. Before a final decision was reached D1002-4 were finished in standard green livery with red backgrounds to the name and numberplates with yellow warning panels. *J. N. Simms*

23

Climbing the final stretch of 1 in 110 to the summit of Hatton bank, an unidentified 'Western' heads a Paddington to Birmingham New Street train on 7 June 1975. With the ranks of Class 52s continuing to decline a decision was made in 1975 to restrict their use to freight duties only. This decision was partly due to the fact that worsening service problems had led to some engines having their train heating boilers declared unfit for use and subsequently isolated. However, in practice, such was the shortage of WR motive power, that a serviceable 'Western' could be pressed into use even on a steam-heated passenger duty. By the following year the remaining members of the class attracted a cult following. Twenty-four were required to work the 1976 peak timetable and enthusiasts flocked to photograph and ride them as they all knew it would be the last summer for the class. Ironically, on at least one occasion towards the end of the timetable, the 'Westerns' achieved the BR engineers' dream — 100 per cent availability — with not one being stopped for maintenance or repairs. In perspective, spares were in abundance from the large numbers of condemned locomotives; nevertheless it was an impressive achievement for the remaining 24 members of the class. *Ray Reed*

A rare steam-diesel combination is seen here on 20 September 1963 as the pioneer D1000 *Western Enterprise* pilots an unidentified Stanier '8F' 2-8-0 on the climb to the summit of Hatton bank. Together with D1002/4/5, D1000 had been allocated to Oxley MPD from 25 June 1962. A fifth member of the class was at Shrewsbury for crew-training on a diagram including the 7.30am Shrewsbury to Wolverhampton and 12.15pm return. *Bryan Hicks*

Below: An unexpected surprise for the photographer who had set out to capture the 'Western Pullman' set as he finds green-liveried D1002 *Western Explorer* heading a rake of old-style Pullman coaches up Hatton bank on 6 June 1963. Frequent failures of the 'Western Pullman' led to its withdrawal from traffic on 13 June 1964 for a period of six weeks while a complete overhaul was undertaken. All of the 'Blue Pullmans' were withdrawn in May 1973 after the new Mk 2 coach designs had surpassed their levels of comfort. *Bryan Hicks*

Right: With the line to Stratford-on-Avon diverging to the left, D1010 *Western Campaigner* heads one of the many final railtours. This tour on 27 November 1976 originated in Plymouth and had taken participants up to Birmingham before returning to Plymouth via Basingstoke. Seven 'Westerns' remained in traffic on New Year's Day 1977, but by the end of January both D1022 and D1058 had succumbed. D1041 *Western Prince* lasted until 22 February leaving D1010/3/23/48 in traffic until the final withdrawal of the type on 27 February 1977. *Ray Reed*

Left: This splendid picture taken between Solihull and Olton depicts D1006 *Western Stalwart* with the 7.40am (SO) Leamington Spa (General) to Birkenhead (Woodside) on 27 July 1963. The 'Westerns' had commenced regular operations on the Paddington to Birmingham route on 25 June 1962, their first diagrams covering the 10.35am Wolverhampton to Paddington and 4.10pm back from Monday to Thursday and the 8.33am Wolverhampton to Paddington and 1.10pm back on the Friday and Saturday.

Above: No D1019 *Western Challenger* is seen passing Bentley Heath level crossing as it restarts the 5.10pm Paddington to Shrewsbury from Knowle & Dorridge station on 25 June 1963. No D1019 was one of the first two 'Westerns' to be withdrawn and was condemned at Laira on 6 May 1973. It was one of four 'Westerns' not included in the dual-braking programme and was taken out of traffic when it required a replacement engine. Within the next three months the remaining three engines without dual-braking were also taken out of service. *Both: M. Mensing*

29

Below: D1035 *Western Yeoman* is in charge of the up 'Cambrian Coast Express' on 17 September 1962 having just passed Acocks Green station in Birmingham. There were no significant differences between the 'Westerns' constructed at Crewe and Swindon. However the detail enthusiast would point out that the location of electrification symbols were placed slightly higher on the Crewe-built machines and Great Western men at Swindon would have said that the Crewe product was easily identified by its rippled body finish.

Right: Another view of the up 'Cambrian Coast Express' near Acock's Green, this time with D1007 *Western Talisman* in charge on 26 September 1963. No D1007 ended its service on BR with a very serious accident which happened between Ealing Broadway and West Ealing at Longfield Avenue on 19 December 1973. It was working the 17.18 Paddington to Oxford when it totally derailed and blocked all four roads. No D1007 fell on its side and remained intact but at least three coaches concertined killing 10 passengers and injuring 50 others. *Both: M. Mensing*

Left: A final view near Acocks Green taken on 3 April 1963 as D1002 *Western Explorer* is in charge of the 8.50am Birkenhead (Woodside) to Paddington. When introduced on this route the WR had stated that in the event of a 'Western' class diesel being unavailable at any time on the accelerated Paddington-Birmingham-Wolverhampton expresses recourse to steam would be avoided. The 'Westerns' had displaced steam on the route when the summer timetable was introduced in May 1962. However, their stay on this line was short-lived for by 1964, when it came London Midland control, the new Brush Type 4s ousted the hydraulics.

Above: The late-running down 'Cambrian Coast Express' approaches Tyseley station on 15 August 1963 behind D1065 *Western Consort*. The reason for lateness on this occasion was due to a fatal collision at Knowle & Dorridge station involving sister locomotive D1040 *Western Queen*. D1040 had been working the 1.0pm Birmingham to Paddington formed of the spare set of Pullman coaches and had run into the rear of a freight which had stopped to attach some car flats. The cab of the diesel was completely wrecked and three railwaymen killed. An inquiry was held on 23 August after several test runs were made on the section of line concerning braking tests. *Both: M. Mensing*

A rear three-quarter view of D1038 *Western Sovereign* as it works away from Tyseley, Birmingham, with the 8.55am Birkenhead (Woodside) to Paddington on 4 November 1962. Initially, D1038 joined Swindon's first batch of nine locomotives D1000-8, at Laira, and Crewe-built D1035/6/7/9, where they were used on the heavy West of England services. Whereas the 'Warships' at Laira were operating on out and back diagrams the 'Westerns' appeared on two-day cyclic diagrams involving a trip to Paddington and then to Birmingham and Wolverhampton where they were serviced at Oxley or Tyseley before returning back to London and finally returning to Laira for maintenance. Whilst being serviced at Oxley or Tyseley they were often found on local passenger turns around Birmingham or even on an overnight parcels working to Swindon. Eventually these diagrams were extended to three days which were similar to the two-day roster except they would operate as far as Chester. Eventually their duties were extended into South Wales in addition to their operation on the West of England and Paddington to Birmingham routes. *Mike Mensing*

Desert Sand-liveried D1000 *Western Enterprise* is about to pass Tyseley station with the 12.10pm Paddington to Birkenhead (Woodside) on 15 March 1963. Surprisingly, as the naming of D1000 at Paddington was supposedly secret, it arrived with the prototype 2,800hp diesel-electric Brush *Falcon* on the 6.55am Cheltenham to Paddington on 20 December 1961, already displaying its name. *Mike Mensing*

No D1013 *Western Ranger* is seen against the buffer stops at Penzance's platform 1 having worked in from Birmingham on 26 October 1976. Together with D1031/62/63, D1013 was the second of the class to be equipped with air-brakes at Swindon in 1968. Prior to that it had been necessary for South Wales trains formed of air-braked Mark 2A stock to be exclusively hauled by Brush Class 47s. With only four months to go before the end of the 'Westerns', BR was losing the last in a line of locomotives that had given the Western Region its individuality. No D1013 was to survive into preservation but in the last six months of 'Western' operations 18 specials had been run, which in the main had been privately organised, but each one had been a sell-out. On the final day of service BR used all four remaining class members on the 'Western Tribute' railtour. D1013 and D1023 were scheduled to work the train throughout with D1010 and D1048 acting as standbys at Bristol Bath Road and later Laira. The tour travelled from Paddington to Swansea via Swindon, returning to Bristol before heading west to Plymouth. In the event the reserve locomotives weren't required and D1023 had the honour of leading the WR's last 'Western'-hauled train into Paddington. *Roger Winnen*

Almost totally devoid of paintwork D1015 *Western Champion* awaits departure from Penzance with the 10.10 Penzance to Paddington on 23 May 1976. Of all the 'Westerns' surviving into preservation the story of D1015 is perhaps the most miraculous. As a partly stripped and derailment-damaged hulk it was rescued from Swindon by the Diesel Traction Group and after extensive restoration it re-emerged in its original Golden Ochre livery in 1982. *Roger Winnen.*

This view taken at Long Rock depot, Penzance, on 27 October 1974 depicts D1059 *Western Empire* with its paintwork quickly disappearing. The coal stage and water tank above was dismantled and demolished during April 1976 and was followed by the rest of the engine shed building during the early summer of that year. Cutting of the first turf for the new depot at Long Rock was carried out by the Chairman of Penwith District Council, Mr Donald Trewern, on 30 March 1976. After widespread rumours had been circulated about the closure of the main line west of Plymouth, Mr Arthur Eplett, BR's Area Manager, reassured those present at the cutting of the turf that it was BR's intention to stay in Cornwall. The new depot included fuelling facilities as well as carriage washing, cleaning and maintenance facilities. D1059 was withdrawn from traffic at Laira depot one year later in October 1975 and after one month in store was despatched to Swindon to be scrapped. *Roger Winnen*

D1023 *Western Fusilier* is seen arriving at Falmouth Docks station with the 'Western China Clay' railtour on 4 December 1976 tailed at the rear by D1056 *Western Sultan*. This tour also visited the Par to Newquay line and the Lostwithiel to Fowey branch. Following an increase in passenger traffic on the Falmouth branch the station at Falmouth Dock, closed in 1970, was re-opened in 1975 when about half a mile of track was brought back into passenger service from the new terminus which was subsequently renamed The Dell. *Roger Winnen*

Left: Climbing the 1 in 68 across Clinnick viaduct, a somewhat scruffy D1018 *Western Buccaneer* threads the Upper Fowey valley away from Bodmin Road with the 10.30am Penzance–Paddington on 27 August 1966. D1018 was never fitted with air brakes and despite a full repaint in the early part of 1973 it was one of the early casualties and was withdrawn in June of that year. Unfortunately many of the classic views along this valley are now hidden behind forestation although recent replanting near Largin viaduct has opened up a view of down trains from the west side of the valley, albeit in a somewhat cramped location. After spending two months at Laira after withdrawal, D1018 was returned to Swindon for breaking, finally meeting the cutter's torch in March 1974. *Peter W. Gray*

Above: D1012 *Western Firebrand* awaits departure from Plymouth North Road station on 3 April 1968 with 1M95, the 11.30am Plymouth–Manchester — the assisting locomotive is 'Warship' D817 *Foxhound*. The new station at North Road was officially opened by Dr Beeching on 26 March 1962. Constructed as part of the re-building of the bomb-scarred city, it had cost an estimated £1,800,000 and had taken six years to complete. At that time it was considered to be the most modern on British Railways and compared favourably with those in mainland Europe. Passengers were catered for with well-designed foyers and a booking hall with refreshment and waiting rooms on all the platforms, the catering facilities including the luxurious new 'Brunel Bar' and cafeteria/waiting room. *Terry Nicholls*

41

Above: Restricted to local working only in Cornwall at that time D1071 *Western Renown* arrives at Plymouth with the stock for 2B24, the 17.30 Plymouth to Penzance on 4 July 1973. As Plymouth was suffering less competition for skilled labour than London, the WR chose to construct its first main line diesel depot at Laira on wasteland adjacent to the old steam shed. It was progressively brought into use and facilities for DMU maintenance were available by October 1960, DMUs having taken over from the steam operated push-pull services in June of that year. *Andrew Wiltshire*

Right: Semaphores are still in evidence in this picture taken on 11 August 1972 as D1028 *Western Hussar* heads a down freight past the signalbox at South Brent. Despite the 'Westerns' being primarily intended for express passenger workings, their design suited their use on heavy freight. Their low weight and braking force restricted their use on the most demanding duties but despite this they performed well on the Scunthorpe to Cardiff steel transfers and on the Somerset quarry trains. Another of their important duties was on the china clay trains between Cornwall and the Potteries. *Peter J. Fitton*

Left: Two views taken on the western climb to Dainton summit. Here, North British Locomotive Co Bo-Bo 1,100hp diesel-hydraulic D6312 pilots D1070 *Western Gauntlet* with the 7.50am Penzance–Paddington on 17 June 1967.

Below: Another view on the same day shows super power for 1M95, the 8.00am Newquay to Manchester and Liverpool, as D1014 *Western Leviathan* and D1045 *Western Viscount* get to grips with the 1 in 55 gradient. *Both: Peter W. Gray*

Left: This picture taken at Stoneycombe on the eastern climb to Dainton summit shows D1001 *Western Pathfinder* climbing the 1 in 46 with 10 coaches forming the down Cornish Riviera Express (10.30am ex-Paddington) on 17 June 1967. Earlier that year D1071 *Western Renown* had been involved in a collision at Bristol East depot. On 11 January the 2.55 Acton–Margam freight had become derailed at Chipping Sodbury, Paddington–South Wales services being diverted via Bath until the 12.00 Paddington–Swansea headed by D1071 ran into the back of the 11.45 Paddington–Bristol blocking the main line. Fortunately the Badminton line was cleared by 15.00 and Bristol trains were diverted via that route. *Terry Nicholls*

Right: D1021 *Western Cavalier* is passing Langford's Bridge near Aller Junction with an up passenger working in June 1969. What was hailed as the zenith of diesel-hydraulic performance came in 1969 with the separation of Torbay and Penzance services, each on a two-hourly pattern (even hours to Plymouth/Penzance and odd hours to Torbay), thus providing Exeter with an excellent hourly service from Paddington. The 'Cornish Riviera Limited' became a nine-coach Limited Load timing with a record 139 mins for the 173.5 miles from Paddington to Exeter, a 74.9mph average speed. Whilst these services were initially entrusted to pairs of 'Warships', by 1971 their reliability was deteriorating and the tight schedules were then entrusted to a single Class 52 or 47. *Peter W. Gray*

For several years the St Austell Motorail with its 'Western' class diesel and long rake of Mk1 coaches, restaurant car and Carflat wagons was a familiar feature of the West of England main line. Here D1011 *Western Thunderer* is passing Aller Junction with a down working on 12 August 1972. The WR had launched its West Country Motorail in 1966, based on the new Kensington terminal. This train ran five days a week with an early morning departure from Kensington. From 1967 it called at Reading to pick up the St Austell portion, then at Totnes to unload Devon-bound cars on to the platform, finally reaching St Austell about 14.00. However, with the extension of the motorway network to the west and with other road improvements, the benefits of using Motorail were reduced. With the introduction of the IC125 units its operation became difficult and in its last two seasons it was confined to running at weekends. When the concept was introduced in the 1950s the Motorail workings conformed to the 60mph average of steam-hauled expresses but on the railway of the 1980s with IC125s it couldn't keep up. *Peter J. Fitton*

An unidentified 'Western' skirts the River Dart at Noss Curve with the 09.58 Newton Abbot–Kingswear on 7 August 1971. With the introduction of the new timetable in 1969 Penzance trains no longer carried portions for the Torbay line, which eliminated the lengthy delays in attaching or detaching coaches on route. The Torbay line was served by four independent through services from London per day and at other times connections were provided from Exeter or Newton Abbot. Travellers using direct services from London on Saturday mornings and early afternoons paid a 10 shilling (50p) supplement which guaranteed them a seat. *P. W. Gray*

Above: A busy scene at Churston recorded on 26 August 1967 as D1032 *Western Marksman* departs with the 16.06 local service from Kingswear to Exeter. D1032 and D1019 were the first of the class to be withdrawn from traffic. Whilst D1019 had not been fitted with dual-braking, the decision to withdraw D1032 after failing a routine examination came as something of a surprise — both locomotives being stripped of reusable parts at Laira.

Right: The 'Western' preservation era has begun, as seen in this picture taken during a Gala Day at Paignton in September 1977. D1013 *Western Ranger* is depicted at the head of a rake of chocolate and cream liveried coaches. Earlier that year, on 20 January, D1013 made what was believed to be the first visit by a Class 52 to Leeds when it arrived with the 07.30 from Swansea. *Both: Peter W. Gray*

Left: This evening view taken at Aller Junction on 21 June 1974 depicts D1069 *Western Vanguard* heading 6B59, the 15.15 Ponsandane (Penzance) to Exeter (Riverside) freight. The first two vehicles behind the locomotive are carrying yellow painted compressors manufactured at the Compair Holman works in Camborne. Class 52 operations at this time were intense, no fewer than 47 members of the class being observed at points between Taunton and Penzance from 15 to 25 April. The WR was too short of motive power to store any locomotive that could work, the Class 52s outnumbering Classes 45, 46 and 47 by five to one although many had a very decrepit external appearance. One exception to this rule was D1023 *Western Fusilier* which, in immaculate condition, worked a special from Swansea to Newport on 6 April. *Les Folkard*

Above: Another evening view taken at Aller Junction, this time showing D1064 *Western Regent* with an up milk train on 5 August 1971. Milk traffic from the West Country was always a regular source of work for the 'Westerns', particularly in later years when they were being displaced from front-line passenger operations. By 1 May 1972 milk trains from the West of England, West Wales and return empties began to work via Acton Yard instead of Kensington. Becoming Class 52 under TOPS, BR decided that with their short life expectancy they should retain their original numbers to the very end and not to assume their new computerised five-digit replacement numbers. Having said that, the 'D' prefix on the numberplates became redundant and in most cases was painted over in the background colour. *Peter W. Gray*

Against a backdrop of semaphores, this view depicts D1017 *Western Warrior* as it gets the right of way to leave Newton Abbot with a westbound passenger train on 4 August 1971. In October 1971 the whole fleet of Class 52s was concentrated on Laira depot in Plymouth and it was generally regarded as the home of the class. After the cessation of overhauls at Swindon in 1973 all repair work was carried out at Laira including swapping reconditioned engines, bogies and transmissions. As the supply of spare parts diminished, locomotives were cannibalised to keep as many of the fleet in traffic as possible. Although the class was being phased out the maintenance staff at Laira understood their idiosyncrasies and arguably the performance and availability of the 'Westerns' had reached their best with low casualty statistics. D1064 soldiered on from Laira until December 1975 where it remained in store, until April 1976 when it was sent to Swindon for disposal, which came in July 1977. *R. C. Riley*

Having only six months to go before withdrawal, D1068 *Western Reliance* was photographed from the sea wall as it passed under the skew bridge at Teignmouth with an up freight on 23 April 1976. The tropical summer of 1976 gave the deboilered Class 52s a chance to reappear on passenger duties. On the nights of 4/5 July and 8/9 July the 21.10 Penzance to Paddington sleeper saw Class 52 power, and on the night of 9 July D1071 *Western Renown* took the 22.35 Paddington–Penzance as far as Bristol, where 50040 took over. This was probably for fuel capacity reasons as the turn involved returning to Par with the ecs. *Roger Winnen*

Below: Another classic view, this time at Dawlish taken from the footpath west of Dawlish station, as D1070 *Western Gauntlet* passes with a westbound working on 1 September 1972. Whilst providing one of the prettiest railway journeys on a sunny day this coastal route often falls victim to savage weather. *G. W. Morrison*

Right: Under a darkening sky D1023 *Western Fusilier* is seen leaving Exeter with the 12.30 Paddington–Paignton on 27 October 1976. As the locomotives approached the end of their careers they were often found carrying their numbers in the headcode panels although officially they should have been set to 0000. *Andrew Fox*

Left: Neglected but not unloved, D1065 *Western Consort* departs from Exeter with an up express in August 1976. From the end of May 1976 no further boiler maintenance was to be undertaken on the remaining 24 operational Class 52s on the Western Region and their long reign on overnight passenger services seemed to be at an end. Although it could be thought that overnight passengers could dispense with heat in high summer, the Region, with a realistic sense of the British climate, preferred locomotives with heating capability for such services. From the date of 'deboilering' a slow decline in the daytime activities of the 'Westerns' became apparent — the class not appearing on the Birmingham services they used to work since the change in the timetable, although they made sporadic appearances on the 11.40 Paddington to Cheltenham and 16.13 return. *T. J. Edgington*

Above: Another view of an up milk train: this time D1011 *Western Thunderer* passes Cowley Bridge Junction, near Exeter, with a St Erth to Kensington working on Sunday 7 May 1967. This train would be booked to call at Dolcoath, near Camborne, Lostwithiel and Saltash as traffic demanded. The loadings varied from four to 15 tanks, each being 14 tons tare weight and 28 tons loaded — the trains returning overnight from Kensington and other bottling depots. In May 1980 this business was lost to road haulage with a dozen or more tankers leaving the creamery at St Erth to join the heavily congested A30 for their long journey to London. D1011 was to survive until October 1975, being withdrawn from Laira, where it was stored for one month, before despatch to Swindon, where it remained until January 1979, before being cut up. *M. Mensing*

Above: Another picture taken at Cowley Bridge Junction on the evening of Sunday 7 May 1967. Here D1045 *Western Viscount* is seen with a down express. When new, this locomotive was nominally allocated to Bristol but was the first of the class to arrive at the partially opened depot at Landore, where it was used on crew training. In February 1963 it had been used on an early morning turn west of Swansea and returned from Carmarthen with the up 'Red Dragon'. Withdrawn in December 1974, D1045, like most members of the class, was broken up at Swindon. Not only did this enable parts salvaged to be used in those engines still in traffic but also maintained work at Swindon at a time when there was little new construction. *M. Mensing*

Right: As work on the construction of the Cullompton by-pass (later to become part of the M5 motorway) proceeds apace an unidentified 'Western' takes a down express towards Exeter on 3 September 1968. By the summer of 1965 the WR had gained sufficient confidence in its hydraulic locomotives to accelerate West of England and Bristol services, together with those to South Wales — this being brought about by the return of the 90mph speed limit for the 'Westerns'. From that year the 'Westerns' went from strength to strength, crews getting more familiar with the driving techniques, realising, for example, that a 'Western' could be driven 'flat-out' on notch 7 virtually from a standing start, thereby giving terrific acceleration. *P. W. Gray*

D1010 *Western Campaigner* is carrying the number 1010 in its train number panel on 13 February 1977 as it pauses at Treherbert on its tour of Welsh Valleys with the 'Western Requiem' railtour. Such was the demand to travel on this tour that the train operating on the 13 February was actually the relief — the main tour running on 20 February. Unfortunately, on this occasion D1010 failed at Cardiff, Class 37 No 37179 taking the tour train up to Treherbert and Aberdare. In the meantime, D1023 *Western Fusilier* was despatched from Old Oak Common to Pontypridd, where it took over up to Merthyr Tydfil and finally back to Paddington. Two years earlier, on 17 March 1975, D1010 had the task of hauling the preserved Stanier Pacific No 6229 *Duchess of Hamilton* on the final leg of its journey from Butlin's Holiday Camp, Minehead, to BREL Swindon, where it was to be restored as a static exhibit in the National Railway Museum at York — D1010 taking over at Taunton.
Terry Nicholls

This picture, taken on 16 August 1975 near Avonmouth, depicts D1055 *Western Advocate* waiting for departure with an empty van train. As described earlier, D1055 was extensively damaged in a fatal collision near Worcester on 3 January 1976. It had worked north with 6M55, the 18.05 St Blazey to Longport clay train. Following the crash the locomotive was removed to the depot at Worcester, where it was to remain until March of that year, when it was taken to Swindon Works for scrapping — final breaking taking place in June 1976. *Andrew Wiltshire*

Above: D1057 *Western Chieftain* is captured on 17 June 1975 as it heads a Swansea express through Pencoed on the South Wales main line. Diesel servicing facilities in South Wales were first provided at the rebuilt facility at Landore, which having closed to steam in June 1961 was partially opened as a diesel depot in February 1963, becoming fully operational in May of that year. However, more important was the decision to provide a major depot at Cardiff Canton. Canton closed to steam in September 1962 with the transfer of its remaining locomotives to East Dock. Work on the new facility was completed by September 1964, services provided including fuelling and sanding points, a washing plant and heavy lifting gear. The depot was responsible for the maintenance of about 200 locomotives. *John Wiltshire*

Right: Carrying the experimental Golden Ochre livery, D1015 *Western Champion* is being prepared to leave Severn Tunnel Junction depot on 19 May 1964. Following closure the depot at Severn Tunnel Junction was acquired by a firm of car transporters for use as a road-to-rail distribution depot for Ford cars, being brought into use on 22 February 1966. The depot received cars by rail for distribution in South Wales and across the Severn Bridge. On 30 January 1965 D1015 had been specially prepared to work the returning empty stock of Sir Winston Churchill's funeral train. By the end of 1965 the locomotive had been repainted in maroon. *J. N. Simms*

Left: This panoramic view of Bristol East depot sees D1013 *Western Ranger* as it passes with a ballast working on 6 February 1977. On 18 February D1010/3/23 all worked light from Laira to Old Oak Common for further railtours. On 19 February D1013 worked the 'Southern Belle' to Dorchester and Weymouth before being deployed on the final day of WR diesel-hydraulic operation with the 'Western Tribute' railtour on 26 February. D1013 passed into preservation when it was purchased privately by a Western Locomotive Association member who entrusted it to the association. Together with D1062 *Western Courier,* it moved to the Severn Valley Railway which was to be their long-term home.

Above: Idling in a smoky haze, D1010 *Western Campaigner* and D1048 *Western Lady* are seen outside the depot at Bristol Bath Road on the final day of WR diesel-hydraulic operation. The pair were standby locomotives for D1013 *Western Ranger* and D1023 *Western Fusilier,* which were deployed on the 'Western Tribute' railtour. The reserve locomotives later stood by at Laira but in the event neither was needed and D1023 was to head the last 'Western'-hauled train into Paddington. Whilst for many it was the end of an era, it was also the end of WR's 1955 vision of the future. All four locomotives used on the last day in traffic escaped the cutter's torch.
Both: Terry Nicholls

Below: Blue-liveried D1015 *Western Champion* is depicted leaving the station at Bristol Temple Meads with the 08.00 to Plymouth on 18 May 1976. Of all the hydraulics to operate on the WR the greatest support was for the 'Westerns', with new fewer than seven examples, including *Western Champion*, surviving into preservation. The massive achievements of the various preservation groups is not to be underestimated: the surviving WR diesel-hydraulics have become valued items of motive power on a number of preserved railways.

Right: Another view taken at Bristol Temple Meads, this time showing D1051 *Western Ambassador* working the 4.05pm parcel van train to Plymouth. This was a regular working with a light load and was often used to get locomotives running on one engine back to Laira for attention. Introduced in 1970, the Multiple Aspect Signalling (MAS) project at Bristol was claimed to be the one of the largest track and signalling modernisation schemes carried out in Europe by that date. This scheme replaced a GWR scheme of 1934-5. *Both: Terry Nicholls*

Left: In this panoramic view taken at Bath on 5 September 1971 an unidentified 'Western' pulls away from the station with the 13.45 Paddington to Bristol. With a programme of permanent way improvements and the MAS signalling, the Bristol and South Wales timetable was restructured and diagrammed exclusively for Class 52 and Class 47 haulage. This culminated in the May 1972 even-interval timetable programmed for D350 (diesel-hauled, load up to 250 tons) timing loads. As air conditioned and electrically heated stock was drafted to the WR, activity by diesel-hydraulic locomotives declined. *Hugh Ballantyne*

Right: This picture taken in July 1976 shows D1005 *Western Venturer* passing under Brunel's Clifton Suspension Bridge with a paper pulp train from Portishead, bound for Bristol's Board Mills at St Annes. An unusual mishap befell D1005 some years earlier and deserves a mention here. It happened on 12 December 1962 when the locomotive was tackling the rising grades south of Cropredy with the 3.10pm from Paddington in a blizzard. It ploughed at about 75mph into a herd of cows, killing six of the beasts. The impact ripped the brake gear from the diesel and the resultant emergency braking effect on the train was of an intensity to cause skidding and to wear several 'flats' on the carriage wheels. The train was eventually brought into Birmingham some two hours late after D1005 had been removed to Banbury shed. *Terry Nicholls*

An early picture of maroon-liveried D1053 *Western Patriarch* taken east of Keynsham on 13 May 1964 as it heads the 4.33pm Weston-super-Mare to Paddington. The initial performance of the 'Westerns' was mediocre, the failure rate high, the running disappointing, and, without warning, there was an outbreak of metal fatigue in the axles. With the 'Warships' suffering excessive flange wear, a temporary restriction of 80mph was imposed by the WR for a few months, the 'Westerns' also being restricted. By the summer of 1965 the WR had summoned sufficient confidence to accelerate its West of England and Bristol services and returned to a 90mph speed limit for the 'Westerns'. From that year the 'Westerns' went from strength to strength and like so many diesel types their performances improved as time passed. In many ways the early performance of the 'Westerns' gave them a poor reputation and when the ex-GWR main line north of Birmingham became the responsibility of the London Midland Region they were quickly dismissed in favour of the Brush-Sulzer Type 4s. *M. Mensing*

During the course of the 1970s materials for construction became an increasing source of revenue for British Rail and in particular the Western Region. One aspect of the 'Westerns' operation was their early use on slow, heavy goods workings. With their greater weight and braking force they were better suited to these operations than the other diesel-hydraulics. Here, D1005 *Western Venturer* is pictured near Blatchbridge Junction with stone empties on 12 August 1972. *Peter J. Fitton*

This picture of D1006 *Western Stalwart,* taken at Gloucester on 27 November 1965, coincided with the occasion of the last steam train from Paddington hauled by No 7029 *Clun Castle.* The immaculate D1006 was used on the return run to Cheltenham St James before 7029 worked the train from Gloucester Central to Swindon. As can be seen in this view D1006 was the subject of an experiment with circular action marine-type wipers. Also fitted to D1039, they proved effective in keeping the glass clean, but due to their complexity and size they were deemed unsuitable for use on the whole class. Another trial using horizontally moving windscreen wipers fitted on the driver's side only and mounted on the bottom of the screen was implemented on four other 'Westerns'. As with the rotary wipers this scheme was not implemented on other members of the class. *T. J Edgington*

D1054 *Western Governor* is illustrated here as it heads an up express east of Didcot on 3 November 1965. Together with D1055/56, D1054 was in the latest batch of 'Westerns' to be allocated to Cardiff Canton when new in March 1963. However, they were first sent on loan to Tyseley for crew training, other examples of Canton's allocation which hadn't arrived being D1044 *Western Duchess,* which was at Salisbury, and D1045 *Western Viscount* at Landore. D1044 was at Salisbury with a view to its use on through workings from Cardiff to Portsmouth and Brighton in the summer timetable. *Bryan Hicks*

Green-liveried D1037 *Western Empress* heads an up freight through Sonning Cutting on 11 May 1963. By the time this locomotive's repaint was due in early 1967, the green paintwork was looking decidedly tatty, it being repainted in blue livery, albeit a pale shade with metallic pigment. D1037 was one of only three class members not to carry the maroon livery. The first member of the class to receive the blue livery had been D1030 *Western Musketeer* in late 1966. With red bufferbeams and small yellow warning panels it wore an experimental scheme of Chromatic Blue. D1037 along with D1017/36/43/7/57 had joined D1030 in this garb, except that they had been given black bufferbeams. However, March 1967 saw the discontinuation of the experiment in favour of standard Rail Blue with full yellow ends. *J. N. Simms*

Blue-liveried D1029 *Western Legionnaire* approaches Twyford on 25 July 1969 with the 16.55 Paddington to Cheltenham. The original nameplates fitted to D1029 read *Western Legionaire*, revised plates being fitted during 1969, possibly using the original plates with the additional letter 'let-in'. D1029 was actually the last member of the class to enter traffic, being retained by the works' Research and Testing section. *T. B. Owen*

Above: A fascinating picture taken on 24 March 1962 near White Waltham shows two newly constructed locomotives working side by side. D1002 *Western Explorer* heads a down parcels and alongside Beyer Peacock (Hymek) Ltd 1,700hp Bo-Bo D7024 heads a down Pembroke train. From 9 to 14 April 1962 was Western Railway Week in the Birmingham Area. An example of the motive power promised for the new 1hr 55min services to Paddington was on view in the north bay at Snow Hill station — this being D1002. Other exhibits included Cafeteria Car M270 and Camping Coach W9887W. *T. B. Owen*

Right: The well organised open day at Laira depot on 15 September 1991 saw the largest selection of diesel-hydraulic motive power assembled since preservation. No less than five out of the seven preserved 'Westerns' were to be seen. Here, lined up for photographers, are D1015 *Western Champion*, D1023 *Western Fusilier* and D1062 *Western Courier.* Now it is the private railways that play host to the surviving WR 'Western'diesel-hydraulics and visitors to these railways can once again hear their favourite locomotives at work. *John S. Whiteley*

Index of Locations

Ian Allan
PUBLISHING

Full details of Ian Allan Publishing titles can be found on www.ianallanpublishing.com or by writing for a free copy of our latest catalogue to:
Marketing Dept., Ian Allan Publishing, Riverdene Business Park, Molesey Road, Hersham KT12 4RG.

For an unrivalled range of aviation, military, transport and maritime publications, visit our secure on-line bookshop at www.ianallansuperstore.com

or visit the Ian Allan Bookshops in

Birmingham
47 Stephenson Street, B2 4DH;
Tel: 0121 643 2496;
e-mail: ia-birmingham@btconnect.com

Cardiff
31 Royal Arcade, CF10 1AE;
Tel: 02920 390615;

e-mail: ianallancar@btconnect.com

London
45/46 Lower Marsh, Waterloo, SE1 7RG;
Tel: 020 7401 2100;
e-mail: ia-waterloo@btconnect.com

Manchester
5 Piccadilly Station Approach, M1 2GH;
Tel: 0161 237 9840;
e-mail: ia-manchester@btconnect.com

and (aviation and military titles only) at the **Aviation Experience, Birmingham International Airport**
3rd Floor, Main Terminal, B26 3QJ;
Tel: 0121 781 0921
e-mail: ia-bia@btconnect.com

or through mail order by writing to:
Ian Allan Mail Order Dept.,
4 Watling Drive, Hinckley LE10 3EY.
Tel: 01455 254450.
Fax: 01455 233737.
e-mail: midlandbooks@compuserve.com

You are only a visit away from over 1,000 publishers worldwide.